AF382267

# HEALTHY EATING

## Simple steps for a more balanced diet

Written by Véronique Decarpentrie
In collaboration with Antonella Delli Gatti
Translated by Emma Hanna

Health and Wellbeing  50MINUTES.com

I rarely have the time to cook. How can I eat more healthily?

Are "light" products better?

I tend to binge when I am stressed or upset. How can I control my cravings?

Is it much more expensive to eat healthily?

I eat healthily but I am not losing weight. What should I do?

Should I cut out all of my unhealthy eating habits?

Do I have to go vegetarian in order to eat healthily?

I have irritable bowel syndrome. Should I avoid eating fruit and vegetables?

## FURTHER READING 81

# HEALTHY EATING

## EAT HEALTHY, BE HEALTHY!

- **Problem:** processed food, combined with our modern lifestyle, has led us to neglect our fundamental nutritional needs and is having a negative impact on our physical and mental wellbeing.
- **Aims:** to identify unhealthy snares and rediscover healthy eating habits in order to keep your body and mind healthy.
- **FAQs:**
  - I rarely have the time to cook. How can I eat more healthily?
  - Are "light" products better?
  - I tend to binge when I am stressed or upset. How can I control my cravings?
  - Is it much more expensive to eat healthily?
  - I eat healthily but I am not losing weight. What should I do?
  - Should I cut out all of my unhealthy eating habits?
  - Do I have to go vegetarian in order to eat

healthily?

- ◦ I have irritable bowel syndrome. Should I avoid eating fruit and vegetables?

Fatigue, a dull complexion, bloating, chronic pain, obesity and so on are all signs that our body is not working properly. However, we often choose our meals carelessly, disregarding the potential negative effects on our health and without knowing what really goes into our food. Why are we so out of touch with our body's basic needs? What should we do in order to eat more healthily?

Our cravings, habits and even our emotions are influenced by the food we eat. In just 50 minutes, you will learn to recognise what the driving forces behind your dietary choices are and how to avoid falling into the traps of unhealthy eating habits. You will also learn about positive habits which will introduce you to a whole new world of healthier culinary delights. Regain your energy, lose weight and improve your physical and mental wellbeing with this helpful guide!

# OUR CONSUMER SOCIETY

"I'm a mother of three and I would like to cook more balanced meals for them, but by dinnertime I'm mentally and physically exhausted and I never have the energy to cook anything other than pasta in tomato sauce." (Amanda, 42)
"I know that I eat very badly, but even though I'm aware of it I can never change my habits!" (Julian, 22)
"I would like to feel healthier but there are so many different options – high-protein diets, low-carb diets, raw food diets and so on – that I feel totally lost and I have no idea which one to follow!" (Carol, 26)

## THE POWER OF UNHEALTHY EATING

Even though there is no shortage of food in Western countries nowadays, the question of which food to eat has never been more topical. Lack of time, (compulsive) cravings, stress, the wide variety of food on offer and addictive additives often lead us to make unwise dietary choices and form habits which can be difficult to break. Likewise, illnesses which are directly related to our diet, such as obesity, diabetes and high blood pressure, are having an ever-greater impact on our health. Hippocrates, who famously said "Let food be thy medicine and medicine be thy food", would be turning in his grave if he could see us now.

There seems to be no escaping the idea of getting your five portions of fruit and vegetables a day, and television, magazines, the internet and adverts are constantly bombarding us with their own advice, opinions and recommendations, not to mention all the new diets which are constantly popping up and promising to change our lives. The processed food industry has also played a central role in this crisis, offering us products emblazoned with advertising slogans that proclaim them to be "low in saturated fat" or "a great source of calcium", or any number of other nutritional buzzwords. But can we really trust what they say?

If you feel like you are drowning in a sea of contradictory messages, you are certainly not the only one. In this book, we are going to take the time to examine the processes which have alienated us so completely from our fundamental nutritional needs. Anyone can see that junk food can even overpower our common sense, so we need to ask what is really going on both inside our body and around us.



## THE WORLD AROUND US

In this globalised era, trading with the other side of the world has become commonplace. The days when our meals came from no further away than our own vegetable gardens and the local grocery store are long behind us (in spite of small-scale attempts to revive these habits). Of course, in bygone eras people relied heavily on seasonal produce and had to put up with very repetitive fare – it is not difficult to imagine them saying "Oh wow, potatoes again!" in deeply sarcastic tones.

Today it is commonplace to see miles of shelves stacked to the ceiling with countless multi-coloured products, but this was unheard of until the 1960s. Globalisation has made our daily lives incredibly comfortable thanks to the astounding variety of food that it offers us, but we should never forget that this abundance also comes with drawbacks, especially for our health and digestive system – to say nothing of the immense quantities of waste that are produced as a result.

# WHAT REALLY CONTROLS OUR BODIES?

## THE BRAIN: A DEPENDANT ORGAN

Our body is naturally programmed to prefer fats and sugar; in fact, children are innately drawn to them, and breastmilk is rich in both. These two nutrients are essential, and keep our body working properly. Glucose, a type of sugar, is even the main source of energy for our brains, which consume around 120 g of glucose a day on average (around half of our recommended daily allowance). Also, did you know that the membrane surrounding every cell in your body is made of fat?

Bearing these facts in mind, it is hard not to wonder why these two basic nutrients have such a terrible reputation in this day and age. So many of us have a "sweet tooth" and find it extremely difficult to resist indulging it, and certain studies even compare sugar to cocaine or heroin to emphasise just how addictive it can be! Meanwhile, endless studies claim that fats are the cause of any number of diseases, as well as our bodies' curves.

Our cravings for these two nutrients are rooted in pleasure. Both fats and sugar directly fulfil some of our bodies' fundamental needs, and they stimulate the reward centres in our brain, which releases dopamine (a neurotransmitter associated with pleasure). This is why it feels so good to have a little piece of chocolate, and combined with the stress of modern life, it can become an irresistible temptation. This means that bitter, sour or spicy flavours can be very useful, as they can help us to control our sugar cravings.

### ARE YOU ADDICTED TO SUGAR? TAKE THE TEST AND FIND OUT!

Are you in control of your sugar cravings, or do they control you? Who is stronger? To find out, take this test: try to cut out all processed sugar (fizzy drinks, chocolate bars, biscuits, cakes, etc.) for a whole day.

You should also be careful with foods which do not seem sugary, but which do have hidden sources of sugar, such as canned vegetables, bread or breakfast cereals, which can be extremely high in sugar.

Pay close attention to how you feel and track your own reactions meticulously. The next day, read over your results to get an idea of how much power sugar wields over you.

- **No dependence:** if you felt a craving for sugar but overcame it and ate something else instead.
- **Slight dependence:** if it was difficult for you to resist the craving but you still managed to overcome it.
- **Average dependence:** if you gave in and you know it. It is time to change your habits.
- **Strong dependence:** if you could not resist temptation and you made up excuses to justify giving in. Sugar totally controls you, and it will be a tough struggle to break free of it. Start by replacing a third of your processed sugar consumption with fruit (strawberries, apples, oranges) and

gradually increase this proportion, and try to gradually replace processed sugar with non-sugar alternatives over time.

## OUR INDISPENSABLE INTESTINAL FLORA

Approximately 100 billion bacteria from over 400 different species reside in our intestines. Each of these species has its own DNA (each living creature's "ID card"), its own nutritional needs and its own specific role to play in maintaining our health. How much these species flourish depends on the food you consume, and you can even nourish some of them to the detriment of others. As such, it is important to get to know the creatures that live inside us.

These organisms' most important function is to digest the food we eat. They break our food down into nutrients such as vitamins and minerals (components of our food which our body can absorb directly and which play an essential role in keeping our body working properly).

These "good" bacteria also play an important

role in keeping our immune system working properly, and build up our resistance to disease and illness. In fact, their presence alone helps to prevent "bad" bacteria from building up in our gut, as some of them secrete bactericidal substances (a kind of natural antibiotic). They can also neutralise toxins and even fight off viruses.

As such, it is clear that they are formidable allies in the struggle to keep our bodies healthy, so it should come as no surprise that problems with our intestinal flora can lead to a wide variety of illnesses, including obesity. More and more scientists are investigating just how much influence our microbiota (the community of intestinal flora) has on our weight.

Unfortunately, our intestinal flora is quite vulnerable and can be affected by many different factors: even disregarding the alarming impact that medicines, and particularly antibiotics (which have extremely aggressive effects on all bacteria) can have on them, the delicate balance of this flora and its resulting impact on our health is directly affected by the food we eat.

If that were not enough, this intestinal flora also

has a crucial, though lesser-known, effect on our mood. According to recent studies, it acts as a "second brain", and some studies even deem it just as important as our actual brain. Our stomach actually contains millions of neurons (nerve cells which transmit information), just like our brain. These two parts of our body maintain a constant "dialogue", and if one of them starts to have problems, the other will too. For example, if you are deficient in serotonin (a molecule which helps to manage our wellbeing), this can lead to depression, stress and anxiety – and 95% of serotonin is produced in the intestines.

As we can see, our digestive system can have a tremendous effect on our health and mood, but some scientists argue that it also can influence our choices and behaviours. In order to prove this hypothesis, a team of researchers recently began observing two breeds of mice which behave differently: one breed is naturally shy and anxious, while the others are keen, daring explorers, and differences were also found in their microbiota. The scientists then swapped the microbiotas of the two groups of mice, and the results were conclusive: the mice's behaviour underwent a total reversal, with the previously timid breed of mice gaining confidence and vice versa.

It has therefore been proven that these bacteria, like all living creatures, have developed their own biochemical communication system and can even use it to influence our brain.

So, who really decides what you eat? You? Marketing specialists in the food industry? Your intestinal flora? Whatever the case, the power to take back control over your plate and your health is in your hands. In this guide, you will learn about the simple steps you can take to restore the balance of your intestinal flora, as well as the ways you can get back in touch with your basic nutritional needs.

# WHAT DO SUPERMARKETS REALLY PUT ON THEIR SHELVES?

## WHERE DOES OUR FOOD COME FROM?

Prawns which were caught in the North Sea travel an impressive distance to reach our plates: for example, they may travel a total of up to 7000 km from the North Sea to a German consumer's kitchen table, on a route that goes via Morocco for shelling, and then the Netherlands for packaging before finally being delivered to Germany.

Aside from the environmental factors at play, this inevitably raises the question of what kind of impact this journey has on the food's nutritional properties. After all, there is no comparison between a ripe red tomato which has been freshly harvested from your own greenhouse and the bland produce that the supermarkets import from Italy – and given that better tasting food often indicates proportionally higher vitamin content, this raises even more questions. After all, who would choose a tasteless banana over a tasty bar of chocolate?



> **QUICK TIP**
>
> Swap half of your biscuits and chocolate bars for a handful of dried fruit, and swap crisps for cashew nuts. Over time you will see that the less of these unhealthy products you consume, the less power they will hold over you.

## WHAT IS IT?

The food we find on our supermarket shelves is often heavily processed and has had a great deal of other substances added to it. The full scope of the impact that these concoctions can have on our health has not yet been documented, but new debate about them breaks out on a near-daily basis. Some of these additives are considered dangerous to our health, and health experts recommend limiting our intake or even cutting them out altogether.

Aside from their effect on our health, these additives can influence our behaviour by making us crave certain products or by making us feel more or less full than we actually are. The food industry is perfectly aware of the value of these addictive substances and spends millions to create new ones. For example, glutamate, which can be found in stock cubes, sauces and ready meals, is a taste enhancer which stimulates our taste buds and makes us crave food that contains it. These products can wield real influence over us and constantly give us the urge to indulge in junk food.

## WHAT IS IN IT?

Too much sugar, too much salt, and too much fat! These are the three inevitable features of industrially processed food. As we will see, the type of food itself is not the problem – the problems are its quantity, and above all its quality. Junk food professionals know the perfect combination of sugars, salt, fat and proteins that will hit all the right nerve centres in our brains and make us want to eat them again. In other words, we will never be able to get enough of them.

# THE THREE PILLARS OF HEALTHY EATING

## A VARIED DIET

Everyone knows that eating a varied, balanced diet is essential. However, in spite of all the campaigns, television adverts and expert advice that we are bombarded with on a daily basis, it is plain to see that in practice, illnesses which are caused by unhealthy eating habits are more common than ever.

The question is: do we really know how to ensure that our diet features sufficient variety? A varied diet can be quantified by visualising an "ideal" meal, half of which would be made up of vegetables, while most of the other half would consist of carbohydrates and the remainder would be proteins. This allows us to see what our body really needs and how essential it is to ensure variety within these categories.

The food we consume is broken down in our

intestines and falls into three broad nutrient categories: carbohydrates, proteins and lipids (or fats).

## Carbohydrates

Carbohydrates are the main source of the energy that fuels our muscles and brain. Although they are essential, they can also cause many problems (such as obesity, diabetes or high blood pressure) if they are not consumed in moderation.

To illustrate this point, we are going to look at what happens when you drink a can of any carbonated drink. Normally, when we consume sugary foods, the sugar passes into our digestive system where it is broken down into simple carbohydrates which our bodies can process. It then passes into the bloodstream, which raises our blood sugar levels. Our body reacts to this signal by releasing a hormone (a kind of chemical transmitter) called insulin, which facilitates cellular absorption of the sugar, thus reducing our blood sugar levels. It will then either be used to fuel the movement of muscle cells, or stored as fat.

However, in the case of fizzy drinks, the body is inundated with a tremendous quantity of sugar which does not need to be broken down (also known as simple carbohydrates). This means that your body has to release a very large amount of insulin. The whole process is similar to a roller-coaster: blood sugar levels peak because of the drink that was consumed, which is followed by a tremendous crash caused by the enormous quantities of insulin which are needed to deal with this rapidly digestible sugar. Your body will quickly store this sugar as fat, because it will have too much energy available at once. This crash will then renew your craving for "something sweet" to give you another energy boost. This is how people get into the habit of snacking!

Making these complex chemical mechanisms "yoyo" will eventually disrupt the way your body works, which can result in illnesses such as diabetes (a chronic illness which is characterised by an insulin deficiency or by the body being unable to use the insulin it produces correctly).

On the other hand, consuming slowly digestible sugars (known as complex carbohydrates) will prevent your body from going into panic mode, meaning that only a manageable quantity of insulin will be produced and the sugar will remain in your bloodstream for longer. Your muscles will then be able to use up this energy as it is needed.

These easily digestible nutrients are ideal for endurance sports because they will neither raise nor lower your blood sugar levels significantly. Wholegrain cereals (brown rice, wholegrain flour, oats, corn, etc.), pulses (lentils, chickpeas, beans) and most fruits and vegetables are good sources of complex carbohydrates. However, the potential effect on your blood sugar levels will also be affected by the cooking process. For example, a raw carrot has a glycaemic (blood sugar) index of 20, which is bumped up to 50 when it is cooked. Make sure to include some raw food in your diet!

Carbohydrates should make up about half of a balanced diet. Fresh, unprocessed food will be richer in vitamins and minerals and will have much less of an impact on your blood sugar levels. Some of the best sources of carbohydrates include vegetables, cereals and fruit.

- If you find yourself craving something sweet, eat it after your main meal. Combining it with other food will slow down the digestive process.
- Avoid processed foods.
- Reduce your intake of wheat-based products and you will see a corresponding decrease in your sugar cravings.
- Opt for "al dente" rice and pasta instead of overcooking it.
- Opt for fruit instead of juices (even fresh juice) because squeezing the fruit makes it richer in simple carbohydrates and reduces its vitamin content. Try some pulse-based smoothies instead, as they are lower in simple carbohydrates.
- Try using agave syrup, stevia or coconut sugar, as they have very low glycaemic indexes.
- Consider using cinnamon, as it is an excellent blood sugar regulator.

The most important thing is to eat a varied diet within each category. This may seem obvious, but when it comes to cereals, we are often hopelessly unimaginative: practically everything we eat contains wheat. You will find it in your morning toast, in the sandwich you eat for lunch and in the pasta you eat for dinner. More and more people are finding that they feel much better after they reduce their wheat intake (or even cut it out entirely).

In fact, without getting into the debate over gluten (wheat protein) consumption, we do know that everything is a question of balance and proportion. Diversifying the cereals you eat and including quinoa, buckwheat, chestnut, corn, tapioca and other cereals in your diet will help to balance both your health and your moods. You can use these cereals either in their raw form or as flour, which makes it easy to include them in recipes for pancakes, bread, cakes, sauces, and so on.

### RECIPE FOR GLUTEN-FREE BREAD

Ingredients:
- 125 g starch (corn, tapioca or potato)
- 125 g flour (chickpea, chestnut or buc-

kwheat)
- 2 whole eggs
- 2 tbsp extra virgin olive oil
- 1 tsp cider vinegar
- 2 pinches salt
- 10 g yeast
- 1 tsp xanthan gum (to improve texture; can be found in organic stores)
- 220 ml water
- Mix all the ingredients in a large bowl then pour the mixture into a cake tin. Leave to stand for 30 minutes before baking in an oven for 30 minutes at 180°C.

## Proteins

Proteins provide the "building blocks" for our bodies, as they play an essential role in tissue formation. They are also essential for transporting molecules such as oxygen, vitamins and cholesterol. As such, proteins are essential for growth and survival.

So what happens when we consume too much? Aside from the cardiovascular risks associated with consuming the high quantities of fat contained in meat, your kidneys will have to work overtime to filter the substances produced during the digestion of proteins (such as nitrogen).

Furthermore, much of the meat found in supermarkets can contain extremely high quantities of toxins. Opt for organic products instead, as they are both healthier for you and more environmentally friendly.


## DAILY TIPS

- Choose steaks that are no larger than a deck of playing cards (100-130 g).
- Brighten up your plate by pairing your meat with some vegetables or pulses.
- Do not discount wild meats (hog, venison, etc.), as these animals subsist on a natural diet.
- To keep your weekly protein intake balanced, aim to eat meat twice at most (preferably white meat, as it is less carcinogenic), fish once a week (preferably sole, plaice, ray or sardines, as they are less likely to have been affected by pollution due to their smaller size), pulses on two occasions – and why not include an

## Lipids (fats)

Fats play a crucial role in keeping our bodies working normally:

- they are a source of energy;
- they help to transport vitamins (A, D, E, K);
- they help to synthesise a variety of hormones;
- they are the main component of the membranes found in all the cells in our nervous system;
- they play a role in our immune system.

Naturally, this means that attempting to eliminate fat from your diet is inadvisable – instead, you should try to regulate your fat consumption more effectively. There are four broad categories of fats, three of which play a key role in keeping our bodies healthy:

- **Saturated fats**, which can be found in meat, cheese, yoghurt, butter and certain oils such as coconut and palm oil. Generally speaking, these are the fats which get the worst press, because they are associated with "bad cholesterol" and cardiovascular problems, although this link has been contested by a growing number of researchers and doctors. There does not appear to be any real relationship between saturated fat intake and blood cholesterol levels. Conversely, sugar does appear to directly affect cholesterol levels. Nonetheless, as with most things, it is a question of balance: excessive consumption of these fats can lead to obesity and increase the risk of developing inflammatory illnesses such as arteriosclerosis and osteoarthritis (Siri-Tarino et al, 2010).

- **Monounsaturated fats** (also known as omega-9 fatty acids) are the most common natural fats. They can be found in olive oil, sesame oil, nuts, etc. They have many health benefits, including reducing insulin resistance and improving your immune system, among others.
- **Polyunsaturated fats** have been deemed "essential" for our health. Our bodies are actually incapable of producing their own polyunsaturated fats, so our food is our only source of them. They play key roles in keeping your brain and immune system healthy, fighting against allergies and maintaining the

elasticity of your blood vessels and skin. They fall into two distinct categories: omega-6 fatty acids (sunflower, soy, corn, grapeseed and rapeseed oil, etc.) and omega-3 fatty acids (fish, seafood, linseed and walnut oil, etc.). Once again, a good balance is key: excessive consumption of omega-6 fatty acids (which can be found in extremely concentrated doses in industrially processed food) will turn their beneficial effects into harmful effects, as they will effectively replace the omega-3 fatty acids and prevent them from providing us with any benefits. This imbalance can lead to inflammatory problems. Ideally, you should aim to consume two portions of omega-3 for every five portions of omega-6.

## WATCH OUT!

Does the skin on your legs have a bumpy, crocodile-like texture? If so, you almost definitely have an omega-3 deficiency. Incorporate high-quality flax or linseed oil into your diet (making sure to keep it refrigerated and consume it quickly before it turns rancid).

- **Trans fats**, which are partially hydrogenated fats produced as a byproduct of industrial processing, are the only variety of fats which you should aim to eliminate from your diet entirely. They have no health benefits whatsoever and are actually very harmful to human health. Trans fats can be found in pastries, cakes, industrially processed bread, biscuits, chocolate bars and so on – they have become a part of our daily lives. They can lead to cancer, cardiovascular problems, diabetes and a range of other diseases, and have also proven toxic for unborn children and the brain. A recent study also showed that excessive consumption can lead to depression (Sanchez-Villegas et al, 2011).

## DAILY TIPS

The average recommended daily fat allowance is 60-70 g (1 g per kilo of body weight). However, the most important thing is to ensure that you consume a wide variety of sources of fats and, above all, not to neglect omega-3 fatty acids, which are not as common in the foods we eat. Including more of them in your diet is as simple as adding a few different vegetable oils to your larder.

When cooking, opt for sunflower, peanut, grapeseed or coconut oil (because they are more resistant to high temperatures), and use walnut, (extra virgin) olive, rapeseed, linseed or avocado oil as dressing. Do not skimp on the quality or quantity of these oils, as they are extremely beneficial for your health, rejuvenate your skin and, according to certain nutritionists, will not make you gain weight!

## GO ORGANIC

A recent study highlighted the alarming quantity of chemical products which can be found in food produced using traditional farming methods. For example, 100% of the 15 boxes of non-organic muesli (breakfast cereals consisting of a mixture of cereals and dried fruit) studied contained traces of chemicals in quantities which far exceeded the thresholds at which, for example, water is considered unacceptably contaminated (Carrey, 2016).

In addition to their toxic effects, the combination of these poisons is alarming. According to the Belgian Foundation against Cancer, a third of men and a quarter of women will be diagnosed with cancer before the age of 75 – and the numbers are only increasing. Does this mean we should start thinking of cancer as an epidemic?

This raises the question of how large a role these chemicals play in causing other diseases and what effects they can have on our behaviour and our moods. If our gut acts as a second brain, we can only assume that a salad riddled with pesticides and hormones will have disastrous effects on our intestinal flora and on our bodies as a whole.

## The advantages of organic farming

Organic farming is the solution to these problems, because it ensures that the products you buy are toxin-free. But that is not all: the regulations that apply to organic products also specifically ban a number of substances which are considered dangerous to human health. For example, organic foods will never contain hydrogenated fats (which are produced during mass processing when oils are solidified), which can lead to obesity and cardiovascular diseases if consumed in excess.

But organic produce also has even more advantages. As we have already seen, better tasting food often indicates that it is richer in vitamins and minerals:

> "I remember that my mother always used to give me an apple to eat at four o'clock. It was her way of keeping me healthy, so I had to force down the bland, sour apple slices to keep her happy, while she constantly reminded me that "it's good for your health!" It took me years to start eating fruit and vegetables again, but eventually I discovered the joys of sweet, juicy apples at my local organic store, as well as crunchy cucumbers bursting with flavour, and perfectly ripe seasonal tomatoes. Nowadays my chocolate biscuits often seem dull in comparison!" (Amy, 29)

It is no coincidence that organic products are richer in flavour than their traditionally-farmed counterparts.

Organic products have become an essential choice in the modern food market.

However, the organic sector is not immune to the influence of unscrupulous industrial agents who are only out for profit, having seen the popularity of organic products and the potential to take advantage of it. This means that not all brands are of equal quality. Some of these companies simply meet the minimum standards (a lack of synthesised chemical products) so that their products can be certified organic, while others base their entire business models on human and ecological values (fair wages, avoiding deforestation during production, etc.). Research the different brands and their regulations – you will find the logo and means of production on all product packaging, which will provide an indication of what kind of brand it is.

## Go organic without breaking the bank

People often argue that organic food is expensive – but it may not be as expensive as you think. Above all, going organic should be based on four main strategies.

- **Local produce.** Nowadays, organic farming is heavily focused on initiatives promoting local produce, which significantly reduces the food's carbon footprint. Aside from the ethical concerns, this will help you to avoid the products which go through a never-ending series of intermediaries before reaching your plate, which raises prices and is damaging to producers. This means that you will only be paying for your yoghurt, not the marketing and distributor fees which factor into corporate prices.

- **Loose produce.** In recent years, more and more European organic stores have been increasing their range of products which are sold without packaging. As well as being more environmentally-friendly, these products are easier on your wallet. See for yourself – compare the prices of loose spices, flour, dried fruit, etc. by the kilo with their packaged equivalents. Furthermore, this will help you to better manage the quantities you need and to avoid filling your cupboards to bursting, which will help you to avoid unnecessary food waste.
- **"Homemade" produce.** Ready meals, pre-prepared sandwiches, biscuits and so on are generally very expensive. For example, packets of grated carrots are sold at a price that is four or five times more expensive per

kilo than raw carrots. Going organic is first and foremost about reducing your consumption of processed food – but the improvement in flavour will be more than worth it!

- **Get creative.** One of the first habits that you should change is to redistribute your protein intake. After all, there is nothing easier than cooking a piece of meat, but in addition to being expensive, experts say that too much meat (and by extension, too much saturated fat) can be harmful to your health (by increasing the risk of cardiovascular diseases, obesity and so on). Furthermore, more and more plant-based alternatives are appearing on the market all the time, and pulses (such as beans, peas, chickpeas, lentils, etc.) are a cheap, healthy source of protein. Are you intrigued? Try this recipe!

### RED LENTILS WITH YOGHURT, CURRY, HONEY AND LEMON SAUCE

Ingredients:

- 200 g red lentils (bought loose)
- 1 red onion

- 1 tsp curry powder
- 1 tbsp fresh coriander
- Juice of half a lemon
- 100 g natural yoghurt
- 2 tbsp olive oil
- 1 tsp honey
- 1 tsp sesame seeds
- 1 pinch salt and pepper
- Rinse the lentils and cook them in a saucepan of boiling water for 15 minutes. Brown the chopped onion in a frying pan with a little oil. Mix the yoghurt, honey, curry power, lemon juice, olive oil, salt and pepper in a large bowl. Place the lentils in the centre of a large plate and pour the sauce over it. Sprinkle fresh coriander and sesame seeds on top and serve.

You might be thinking that this all seems very well, but that you do not have the faintest idea of where to start. Do not fret – going organic is not something that you need to do overnight. Start with a few products that you use regularly, and then gradually branch out. Let your curiosity guide you, and check out organic shops which sell products that cannot be found in supermarket chains. You will be surprised by how creative these shops can be and discover new flavours in the process.



## IN PRACTICE

The best organic food to buy includes:

- Fruit and vegetables with edible skins, because the majority of the pesticides are concentrated in the skins.
  - **Salads.** According to a recent report published by the French charity Générations futures, traces of pesticides are present in 80% of the salads we eat. 16% of those pesticides are actually banned in France because of their high toxicity.
  - **Strawberries.** Although they are a tasty snack, strawberries are often treated with captan-based products. Even a tiny dose of this fungicide is enough to kill a fish.
  - **Apples.** Conventionally-grown apples are generally treated with a number of chemical products. These substances

are concentrated in the skin, but apples have such thin skin that the toxins can leech through to their flesh.

- Meat, because the tremendous quantities of water (around 15 000 l) and feed (around 7 kg) which are necessary to produce a kilogramme of meat, as well as the horribly unsanitary conditions that the animals are raised in, mean that intensive farming techniques have a great number of harmful effects for both consumers and for the environment, including diseases. To combat these diseases, we are prescribed huge quantities of antibiotics. This combination of antibiotics and the hormones and pesticides found in our food creates a cocktail of toxic chemicals which enters our body every time we eat meat.
- Eggs and milk, for the same reasons as those stated above.

See for yourself: choose a fruit or vegetable which you are particularly fond of, which is in season and does not need to be cooked. Buy a non-organic specimen from a supermarket and another from an organic store of your choice. Cut them into slices and then place them into two bowls, which should have labels on the underside to indicate which is which, then ask a friend or family member to shuffle the bowls so that you do not know which is which. Taste the difference and get your friends to try them too!

## ADD A SPLASH OF COLOUR TO YOUR PLATE

The range of food that nature has to offer is as colourful as it is nutritious – there is nothing stopping you from creating beautifully vibrant dishes that will delight your body, your taste buds and your eyes alike.

Each colour corresponds to a specific health benefit.

- **Red:** foods like tomatoes, watermelons, cherries, strawberries, redcurrants, raspberries, pomegranates, and so on owe their colouration to lycopene, the most powerful antioxidant. Antioxidants track and destroy free radicals which latch onto our cell membranes and cause cancer and premature aging.

- **Yellow/orange:** pumpkins, yellow peppers, carrots, sweet potatoes and apricots are your greatest allies when it comes to resisting illness. Furthermore, these pigments are rich in vitamin A, which will improve your vision and keep your skin and complexion healthy and glowing.
- **Green:** chlorophyll is a green substance which enables plants to transform sunlight into energy. This means that eating green foods is a bit like eating pure sunlight, and thanks to their incomparable "detox" effects, they will make you feel much healthier. The greenest vegetables (chard, spinach, chives, parsley, etc.) have an unmatched power to eliminate toxins (such as those produced by stress, tobacco, alcohol, junk food, etc.) which are the leading cause of tiredness.
- **Purple:** this colour corresponds to intelligence, memory and vision. It indicates the presence of antioxidants and anthocyanosides which preserve the resistance and elasticity of the body's tiniest blood vessels and keep the brain

and eyes hydrated. Blueberries are generally considered a superfood and are rich in these properties, but you can also find them in beetroot, black grapes, red cabbage, Vitelotte potatoes, etc.

- **White:** this category includes onions, garlic, turnips, leeks, cauliflower, asparagus, etc. These foods are rich in vitamins, sulphur and allicin, which regulate certain bodily functions (respiration, joints, anti-inflammation, among others) and can protect against a variety of cancers.

# OUT WITH YOUR OLD HABITS, IN WITH THE NEW

## TOWARDS HEALTHIER HABITS

> "I decided to change my eating habits and at first my colleagues found it all a bit strange. However, they were so intrigued by my colourful, tasty salads that they ended up starting the same diet too!" (Lydia, 34)

Eating is a social act and a way of letting your personality shine through. It allows us to define ourselves culturally, in a family context and personally, while also allowing us to discover and explore the world by broadening our culinary horizons.

Discovering new food and new cooking methods is a challenge which cannot be mastered over-night. You will not be able to replace everything in your kitchen cupboards with wholegrain cereals and leafy vegetables in a single day, but over time, let your curiosity lead you to markets and organic food stores, and fill up a few mason jars with your finds (opting for small quantities of loose products when possible). Try new, healthy recipes that will tickle your taste buds; the simplest things are often the most effective, such as adding a handful of pumpkin seeds to your soup, sprinkling a handful of seaweed flakes over your salad, drizzling walnut oil over your pasta, etc.

And do not forget to use spices, as they are your ticket into a whole world of flavours. As well as giving your culinary creations a unique touch, they also play a vital role in keeping your body healthy.

## THE POWER OF SPICES

Did you know that the vibrant orange spice turmeric has powerful anti-inflammatory and anti-aging properties? Or that cumin is incredibly good for digestion? Or that thyme and rosemary are excellent for helping to fight against viruses and microbes? All of these spices contain valuable substances which act as a great defence against diseases such as cancer.

Eating a more balanced diet and opting for a healthier lifestyle are simple matters. To prove it, we have put together an example of a "well-being menu" below (for adults only, as children have different nutritional needs) which you can put into practice on a daily basis.

- **Breakfast:** a mixture of various cereals, dried fruit and nuts with coconut milk, or an omelette with a tasty slice of gluten-free bread. Pair it with tea or coffee. Avoid:
  - overly bitter or sweet orange juice, as this can irritate your stomach;
  - a simple slice of toast and jam, as it will be digested too quickly and you will start to feel peckish around mid-morning;
  - coffee with milk, which is difficult to digest.
- **Lunch:** a mixed salad (lettuce, apple chunks, cashew nuts, quinoa, dried tomatoes, raisins, walnut oil, etc.). Avoid sandwiches full of saturated fats, as they will leave you feeling drowsy after eating.
- **Mid-afternoon snack:** the fruit of your choice. Avoid chocolate bars or biscuits which are packed with fast-acting sugars.
- **Dinner:** a fillet of fish or meat, paired with a

homemade sauce (made with oil, cider vinegar, soy sauce, mustard, etc.), carbohydrates and two or three different vegetables of your choice. Avoid eating late (make sure that you will have two or three hours to digest your meal before you go to bed) or you may have trouble sleeping.

The most important thing is to find a rhythm that suits you, as this will help you to avoid snacking.

You may have noticed that, unlike many of the diets which pop up everywhere, we have not mentioned dairy products. You should not necessarily cut them out completely, because they are very tasty, but it is important to consume them in moderation. The simple truth is that they are very difficult to digest, because they are designed to facilitate weight gain: a calf which is only fed on milk will gain 200 kg in the space of a year.

"But don't we need calcium to keep our bones healthy?" you may ask. Osteoporosis (loss of bone density which can lead to fractures) is a typically Western disease: in countries where dairy products are rarely consumed, osteoporosis tends to be less common. The scientific community has not yet managed to find an explanation for this paradox and is divided over the role played by dairy products. Although they are not harmful in and of themselves, they undergo a great deal of processing before they reach our plates, unlike in our grandparents' day. These processes are presumably the reason why they are so difficult to digest.

Nonetheless, proceed with caution, because these new habits will never feel natural unless you put your own enjoyment first!

## PLEASURE COMES FIRST

Eating should always be a pleasant experience which creates a feeling of wellbeing and delights the senses – sight, smell and taste, specifically. It is also a time that we can set aside each day to relax and socialise. The joy of cooking is followed by the pleasure of eating, and then by the feeling of contentment that follows a satisfying meal. Try to consider each of these steps equally important or your new habits will never become second nature.

> "I've started to feel much better since I re-evaluated the way I view cooking and eating. My new approach doesn't just mean that I have to find new recipes and try to eat a bit of everything; I also find it immensely satisfying. It has become a very relaxing activity which calms my mind and gives me the chance to let my creative juices flow." (Katie, 32)

Of course, you cannot have an enjoyable diet without giving in to temptation once in a while. Eating healthily is not about adhering to a rigid set of rules and turning meals into a source of pressure for both you and those around you. Beating yourself up over every slip would drain the act of eating of all pleasure, and would therefore prove counter-productive in the long run. Like any other social act, eating depends on the context and should always be, first and foremost, an enjoyable experience. When your friends invite you over for dinner, the company is much more important than the amount of sugar or fat in your food. Meeting your nutritional needs should not just be about keeping your body healthy, but your mind too.

## A NATURAL APPETITE SUPPRESSANT

If you get the urge to snack, drink a glass of water with a teaspoonful of unpasteurised cider vinegar or pour a tablespoonful of chia seeds into a large mug of tea or glass of fruit juice and leave this mixture to stand for 15 minutes. The seeds will form a thick gel which will not only ease your hunger while you are waiting for your meal, but will also provide you with a wide range of vitamins, minerals and omega-3 fatty acids.

# EAT WELL, BE WELL!

"Happiness is largely a question of digestion," according to an Ayurvedic saying. As we have already mentioned, we have a "second brain" in our gut which also controls our emotions. And while our emotions can also affect our digestive system, a balanced diet is a surefire way to improve your wellbeing.

These new, healthy habits ought to help you gain a feeling of contentment, a light, supple body and pleasant, useful energy. Be patient and listen to what your body is telling you. Let yourself make mistakes. Over time, these signals will become clearer and easier to interpret. You will learn how to recognise, respect and respond to them, and how to enjoy doing so.

However, trying to follow a particular diet to the letter is not a good idea – your body knows better than your mind. It will tell you when you are full and what food it needs at any given moment, and according to the seasons. Nature is rarely wrong, so it is best to pay attention to it and follow where it leads.

Now it is up to you!

# FAQS

## I RARELY HAVE THE TIME TO COOK. HOW CAN I EAT MORE HEALTHILY?

You do not need to spend two hours in the kitchen every day to follow a balanced diet. There are plenty of quick, simple recipes out there: the trick is to organise your kitchen and your grocery shopping as best you can. Fill your cupboards with dried fruits, dried vegetables like tomatoes, a variety of cereals and seeds (sunflower, hemp, pumpkin, etc.) and nuts (cashew, pecan, assorted mixtures, etc.).

These non-perishable goods will enhance your meals, salads and snacks, and will provide you with a wide variety of nutrients. You should also keep a supply of ingredients which can be prepared quickly in a pinch such as frozen vegetables, which are actually quite rich in vitamins.

# ARE "LIGHT" PRODUCTS BETTER?

As we have seen, fat and sugar can affect our behaviour. Industrial companies will not hesitate to add high doses of sugar to low-fat products which will therefore be less appealing to consumers in order to improve their taste.

However, artificial sweeteners have the opposite effect on our brains. Once the brain receives a message that sugar has been ingested, but with no corresponding caloric intake, it then often demands more in order to counterbalance it. This triggers an uncontrollable urge to snack.

## I TEND TO BINGE WHEN I AM STRESSED OR UPSET. HOW CAN I CONTROL MY CRAVINGS?

Why do we eat more when we are upset? A loss, break-up, sadness and even simple boredom can be difficult to overcome, and we may feel a profound inner emptiness which we then attempt to fill with food. Can we "feed" ourselves on love, joy and enriching experiences?

Do not blame yourself or beat yourself up about

your weakness. Take a moment before you eat these foods and make a note of the emotions roiling through you. Do not judge or scold yourself, simply adopt the role of an attentive observer. Just by acknowledging them, you will be able to coexist with these emotions, and by paying attention to them, they will guide you towards a healthier solution. This is also the principle upon which "virtuous circles" are based: the healthier your diet, the better you will fare during the difficult periods of your life.

## IS IT MUCH MORE EXPENSIVE TO EAT HEALTHILY?

Naturally, if you switch to buying organic versions of the same products, it will be much more expensive. However, if you start choosing different products altogether, opting for those which are not processed and replacing meat with plant-based proteins and non-packaged food, you can greatly decrease the strain on your grocery budget. Furthermore, there are so many nutritional benefits to choosing a healthy, organic diet that it is actually a long-term investment in your own physical and mental wellbeing.

# I EAT HEALTHILY BUT I AM NOT LOSING WEIGHT. WHAT SHOULD I DO?

Firstly, you should check that your diet is sufficiently varied. The quantity of food you eat is not as important as the quality and variety of that food. Most diets will include wheat and dairy products in almost every meal. Without cutting these foods out of your diet entirely, you should add more variety and try not to eat yoghurt more than a few times per week.

You should also vary the sources of fat that you include in your diet, reducing your intake of animal fats (meat, delicatessen products, cheese, yoghurts, etc.) and increasing your intake of plant fats (soy yoghurt, seitan steak, guacamole, fresh rice or oat cream, etc.). Finally, eating a more balanced diet will not help you if you forget to drink enough water and exercise.

## SHOULD I CUT OUT ALL OF MY UNHEALTHY EATING HABITS?

Unhealthy eating habits are not always due to a lack of willpower or a sign of weakness when faced with temptation. Giving in to temptation and snacking or bingeing has the same effect on our bodies as contact with bad bacteria has on our immune systems. If your diet is "too healthy", your body will no longer have sufficient immunity against external attacks. In fact, you will feel poorly and will suffer gastric reflux after eating a meal that is too heavy or too high in fat, as your body will react and try to purge itself of toxins. It will then begin to use a series of useful adaptive and defence mechanisms which can protect you in all kinds of situations, even to help you combat illness. It is all a question of balance, even these bad habits, provided that they do not get out of hand.

## DO I HAVE TO GO VEGETARIAN IN ORDER TO EAT HEALTHILY?

It is up to you to find a diet that suits you, your personal beliefs, your tastes and your specific needs. However, a healthy diet does not necessarily mean that you need to stop eating animal fats. The quantity and quality of the meat, fish, eggs and other animal produce that you eat are much more important. If you are very fond of meat and fish, do not forget to combine them with vegetarian meals which consist of plant-based alternatives.

## I HAVE IRRITABLE BOWEL SYNDROME. SHOULD I AVOID EATING FRUIT AND VEGETABLES?

For those with irritable bowel syndrome (a digestive disorder which causes symptoms such as stomach pains and dizzy spells), it is generally recommended to eliminate insoluble fibres (which can be found in certain vegetables such as cabbages and crudités, certain fruits like apples and pears, and wholegrain cereals) from your diet and to opt for soluble fibres (such as oat bran, barley, etc.) instead, because unlike insoluble fibres, they will form a kind of gel during digestion which is easier on your intestines.

Generally speaking, diseases which affect the

intestines are the only ones which make it necessary to cut certain fruit and vegetables out of
your diet, at least in the early stages. Following
this, it is best to gradually reintroduce different
types of food into your diet one at a time so that
you can rebalance your intestinal flora. Speak to
your doctor about it: the symptoms and pains
associated with this disease can be alleviated
considerably by adopting new eating habits.

# FURTHER READING


## BIBLIOGRAPHY

- Carrey, P. (2016) Le müesli, un bol de pesticides pour votre petit-déj'. *Libération.fr.* [Online]. [Accessed 7 November 2017]. Available from: <http://next.liberation.fr/food/2016/10/11/le-muesli-un-bol-de-pesticides-pour-votre-petit-dej-_1521169?utm_campaign=Echobox&utm_medium=Social&utm_source=Facebook#link_time=1476198524>

- Clear, J. (No date) What Happens to Your Brain When You Eat Junk Food. *JamesClear.com.* [Online]. [Accessed 7 November 2017]. Available from: <https://jamesclear.com/junk-food-science>

- Collins, S. M., Kassam, Z. and Bercik, P. (2013) The adoptive transfer phenotype via the intestinal microbiota: experimental evidence and clinical implications. *Current Opinion in Microbiology.* 16(3), pp. 240-245.

- Fondation contre le cancer (Belgian Foundation against Cancer) website: <http://www.cancer.be>

- Lallemand, C. (2017) Huit aliments bourrés de sucres cachés. Levif.be. [Online]. [Accessed 7 November 2017]. Available from: <http://www.levif.be/actualite/sante/huit-aliments-bourres-

desucres-caches/diaporama-normal-659771.
html#photo=2>

- Lenoir, M., Serre, F., Cantin, L. and Ahmed, S. H.
  (2007) Intense Sweetness Surpasses Cocaine
  Reward. *PLoS one.* 2(8).

- Larousse.fr. (No date) *Nutriment.* [Online].
  [Accessed 7 November 2017]. Available from:
  <http://www.larousse.fr/encyclopedie/medical/
  nutriment/14856>

- Sanchez-Villegas, A. et al. (2011) Dietary Fat Intake
  and the Risk of Depression: The SUN Project. *PLoS
  one.* 6(1).

- Siri-Tarino, P. W. et al. (2010) Meta-analysis of
  prospective cohort studies evaluating the associa-
  tion of saturated fat with cardiovascular disease.
  *The American Journal of clinical nutrition.* 91.

- P. A. (2016) Teenagers drink a bathtub of sugary
  drinks a year. *Aol.co.uk.* [Online]. [Accessed
  7 November 2017]. Available from: <http://www.
  aol.co.uk/news/2016/11/21/teenagers-drink-a-
  bath-full-of-sugary-drinks-a-year-cancer-rese>

ISHIKAWA DIAGRAM
THE BATTLE OF AUSTERLITZ
NETWORKING